CREATIVE CHILDREN LIKE THE ANIMALS OF THE WORLD

Science, art, and nature spring from the pages in this interactive journey that fosters creative thought, respect for the environment, and a curiosity that will last a lifetime!

Written, drawn, and painted by

Michelle

Written, drawn, and colored by

____

ISBN: 1496168550
ISBN 13: 9781496168559
Library of Congress Control Number: 2014904595
CreateSpace Independent Publishing Platform, North Charleston, South Carolina

THANKS

Creative Children Like the Animals of the World is the result of many years of telling my stories to children and their families.

I thank all of them, since they enabled me to develop the stories from the point of view of the children, what interested them, and what made them laugh.

And now I thank you for developing the book even further—because now this book is yours to develop using your own imagination, unique ideas, and creative thinking.

To begin, go back to the cover page of the book, and write in your name as the writer and illustrator of this book. Then, travel through the world of animals and the world of colors:

1. Read the stories and poems, which are all based on facts of nature.
2. Enjoy looking at their paintings, which were created in acrylic and oil colors.
3. Discover interesting facts about the animals in the stories and poems.
4. Color the illustrations. In fact, you can even illustrate the book yourself.

5. *Be inspired by the stories, the poems, the paintings, and all that you've discovered. Draw your own drawings, and write your own stories.*

You'll see in the book that I sometimes speak to you as myself. In these instances, I use blue letters. Green letters indicate places where you can draw, color, and write. The titles of the stories and poems are written in purple, and the titles of the sections that elaborate on the stories are in light blue.

I wish you lots of fun with *Creative Children Like the Animals of the World.* Thank you so much for all the magnificent ideas that you add to the book!

I hope this book will bring you great joy as you open it in twenty, forty, or sixty years, and rediscover your world as a child.

I'd love to receive your comments about the book on its page on Amazon.com. You're invited to visit RaisingCreativeThinkers.com. A special gift awaits your parents there:
The 10 Golden Tips on
How to Raise Creative Thinkers

You can write to me at this e-mail address:
mchll555@gmail.com

Love, Michelle

TABLE OF CONTENTS

MY UNCLE ANGEL

Dear Children,

I'd like to tell you about my uncle Angel. When I was a child, I loved him so much. Well, I love him a lot today as well. But when I was a child, my mom and dad used to take me to visit Uncle Angel every now and then. He had a big yard, where there were many cages with lots and lots of animals: sweet bunnies, parrots, turtles, and even snakes!

I'd like to tell you about the summer I went to stay with Uncle Angel for a few days. The minute I opened the car door, I ran to him and gave him a huge bear hug.

"Uncle Angel, I love you so much, and I love coming here so much!" I cried.

Uncle Angel managed to say, almost shouting, "Be careful!"

Well, I didn't squash Uncle Angel. But I nearly squashed the bunny he was holding in his arms.

"Sorry, sweet bunny!" I apologized as I caressed its fluffy fur.

Uncle Angel smiled and said, "I see you love animals. You know why you love coming to visit me? Because I love nature, and children love nature, too."

"You know, Uncle Angel, I wish I understood exactly what 'nature' meant. It's such a big word."

"This bunny is a gift of nature," Uncle Angel said. I must have gazed at him in wonder because he added, "You know what? Tomorrow we'll hike a little, so that you get a better feel for what nature means."

That night, I went to sleep with excitement rumbling in my belly. *Where is my uncle Angel taking me tomorrow?*
How will he help me to understand what nature is?

Early in the morning, I woke him up. I said, "Hey, come on! Let's go! Let's enjoy the brightness and the glow!"

We walked among trees full of lush foliage, from which birds peeked out to sing their morning songs. Flowers opened to the sun's caresses, and ants went on their way, exploring the fields and gathering seeds.

The sun ruled the sky, brightening our eyes with joy. When we reached the top of a cliff, the endless bright blue of the ocean was revealed to us.

"Uncle Angel," I whispered in awe, "this is all so beautiful. But why have you brought me here?"

Uncle Angel replied with a sigh, "You see all this? It's from nature. It is nature: the sun in the sky, the water in the sea, the trees, the birds, and the ants."

"Why?" I asked.

Uncle Angel said, "Because they were not made by people. People made your books and your dolls. But did people make the sun and the trees?"

"Certainly not!" I said. Then I looked around once more, and I understood what nature was.

All of a sudden, I noticed a duck swishing its way across the shore and diving into the wonders of the water.

"Look, Uncle, a duck!" I cried out with pure delight.

Uncle Angel simply said, "Animals are from nature. You know why? Because they can see and hear; they can taste and feel and smell. They have senses, just like you do!"

"Oh, Uncle, look, what a beautiful flower!"
I interrupted.

Uncle Angel simply continued without being offended. "The flower is from nature, too."

"Nonsense!" I cried out. "The flower is not an animal."

"No," Uncle Angel said patiently. "What I mean is that both the flower and the duck are from nature. The flower is not an animal, but it still needs the light of the sun and the water of the rain to grow, doesn't it?"

"Sure it does," I said. "I've never thought of this. Nature sure is beautiful!"

Dear Children,

Although I've grown up, I still love animals. You know why? Because they are so smart. Cats, for example, lick their fur all day long to clean it—a sort of licking bath.

Ants never wander the fields without a reason. Surely they are on their way to their nests, to give the other ants the message that they have found a good supply of seeds.

A little kitten that's just been born can't see its mother.
But it sure can smell its way to her for food.

We have an enchanting world, don't we? The problem is that many animals are not going to survive because we are not taking good enough care of our world.

In the following stories, I will tell you fascinating things about animals and nature. That way, we'll pave the path to taking better care of the world we live in.

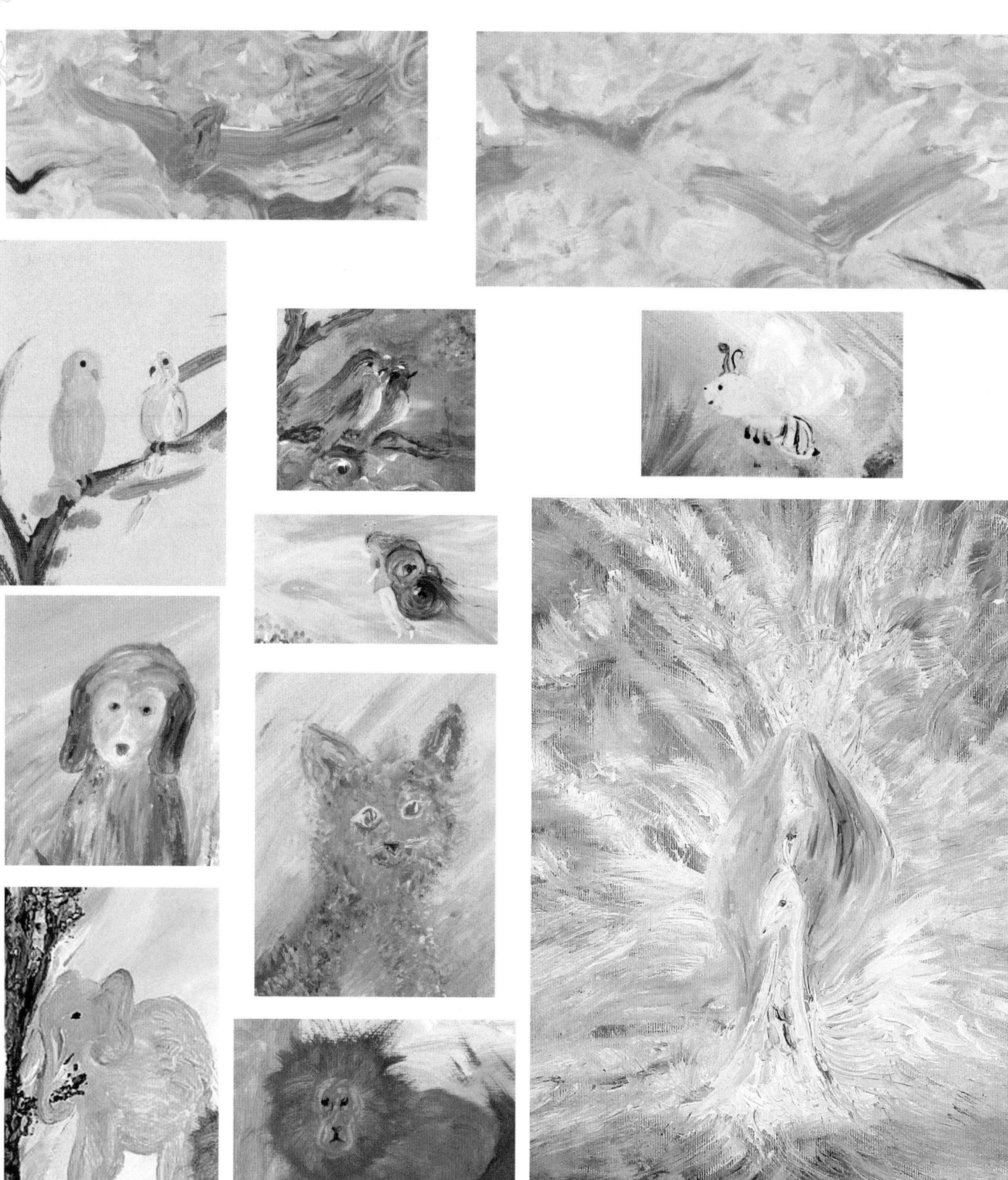

The animal I love the most is...

I love the animals of the world!

SENSATIONAL SENSES

Which is the most important of the five senses?
It's a difficult question, I know.
But I wonder what you think about it.

Sight and hearing are essential, of course.

What about taste and smell? Both are connected, as the mouth and the nose are connected. When we have colds and our noses are stuffed up, there isn't much taste to the food we eat, is there?

If we taste or smell bad food, we know that it is not good for us, and we won't eat it. That certainly protects us from decaying or even poisonous food.

Do smell and taste also protect animals from eating bad food? They do, and therefore they are essential senses for the animals' survival!

What about touch? Why is it important for us?

We actually feel all over our skin, but we feel the most with the tips of our fingers. Amazing, isn't it?

Now, let's say you play ball, fall, and hurt your knee.
A message is immediately sent through the nerves to

the "computer" in your head— your brain. The brain analyzes this message and tells you to take care of the wound.

What do you say? Hasn't touch protected you from being wounded even further? Therefore, it's a very important sense.

What do you think? Did you feel the pain before the message reached your brain?

I'm afraid you didn't. We need our brains to analyze the messages sent by our senses.

Let's say you are ill, running a temperature, and feel awful. Then your grandparents arrive to visit, bringing a present: a new toy!

What miraculously happens? You are bright and happy and even run around with your new toy!

Has that ever happened to you? What happened, exactly?

You were still ill, but your brain was focused on something other than the messages from your senses. You were focused on the new present, and didn't feel the illness at all.

I'd like to suggest something: When you eat, try to taste the food for a few seconds before swallowing it.

We don't taste all of the tastes at the same time. First we taste the sweetness of the food. That's probably why we like sweets so much!

Last to be tasted is the bitterness of the food. How many people do you know who prefer bitter food?

How many children?

No, you don't have to get used to bitter food. You just need to get used to savoring the tastes of the food a bit more. Who knows? Maybe new foods will surprise you with appealing tastes.

To conclude, remember the question we asked earlier: "Which is the most important of the five senses?" Who said that there should be only one answer to every question?

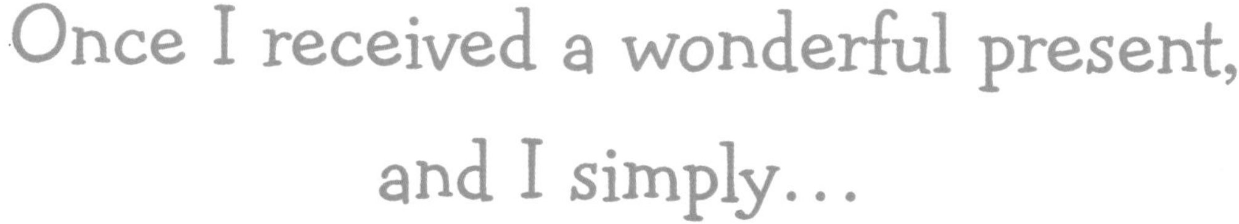
Once I received a wonderful present,
and I simply...

CUTE AND CUTER

Once upon a time, two tiny butterfly eggs were attached to a bud atop an old tree amid a peaceful, colorful forest.

One spring afternoon, a yell was heard from inside one of the eggs: "I'm going to hatch first!" Then a yell was heard from the second egg: "Dream on! I'm going to be first!"

Cute was the first caterpillar to hatch. He was one hour older than his brother Cuter, the second caterpillar.

The two caterpillars smelled the wondrous smell of the leaves, and became very hungry.

"I'm going to be the first to eat!" Cute said with a shout.

"No way! I'll be first!" Cuter said with a pout.

"You're going to be second!" Cute cried out.

"No, you're going to be second!" Cuter said without doubt.

The two brothers began to eat, and the eating went on for quite a few days. They ate leaves for breakfast. For lunch, they ate...leaves. And for supper, they ate even more leaves. They ate and they ate and they ate. They grew bigger and bigger and bigger. Until one day, the feast simply ended.

"Okay, listen. I'm going to pupate first!" Cute said.

"No, I'm going to be first!" If Cuter could blush, he would've felt his face flush with anger and become red.

"No, I'm going to pupate first," Cute had to insist.

"No, you're going to be second," Cuter couldn't resist.

"You know what?" said Cute desperately. "You're first!"

"No way," Cuter said without hesitation. "You're first!"

They probably would have gone on arguing if Cute hadn't begun pupating. Soon he was safely wrapped in a very long silk cord known as a cocoon, and went to sleep.

Cuter didn't have much time to wallow in his distress.
An hour later, he was wrapped in a silky cocoon himself.

Several weeks passed. And one glowing morning, two beautiful butterflies emerged from their cocoons. Cute and Cuter not only became butterflies; they also became mature brothers. They no longer argued all day and all night.

When the sun ruled the sky, they visited beautiful flowers. They feasted on delicious sweet nectar. When the sun was down, they wove splendid dreams. They cherished their time together.

Butterfly eggs can go through a diapause (resting) time. The caterpillars will hatch once the plant they need for their nutrition blooms.

Dear Children,

I've named this painting *Two Who Are One.*
Do you have your own name for it? Write it down here:

____

Do you think there is a difference between being brothers or sisters and being friends—even best friends?
Remember, being brothers and sisters is like being super friends. It's a degree above being friends.

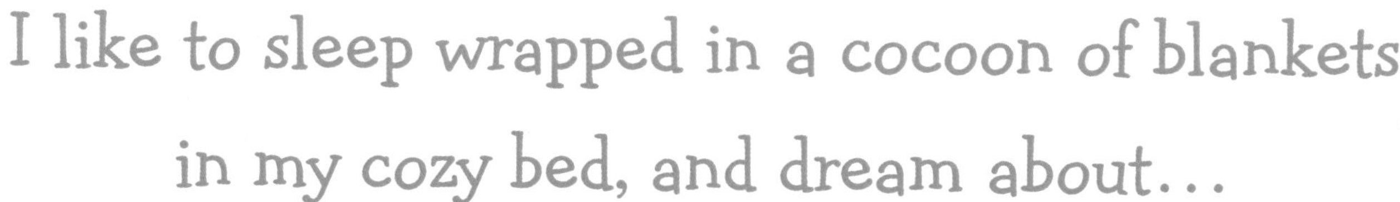

I like to sleep wrapped in a cocoon of blankets in my cozy bed, and dream about...

ITS ALL ABOUT EYES

Why do certain animals have "eyes" on their bodies?

The butterfly has unique, little eyes.

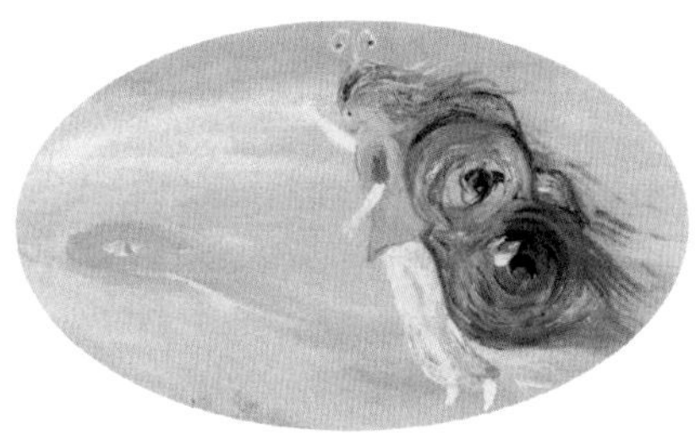

Why, then, do certain butterflies have the shapes of eyes on their wings? What do you think, children? I bet you have a theory.

When a predator intends to catch a butterfly, it wants to succeed on the first try. There may not be a second chance. So it would rather aim for the head of the butterfly.

Certain butterflies trick their predators. They have the shapes of eyes on their wings. The predators will aim for the wings, and damage only them. The body of the butterfly will remain whole, and it will be saved.

It's all about communication between animals.

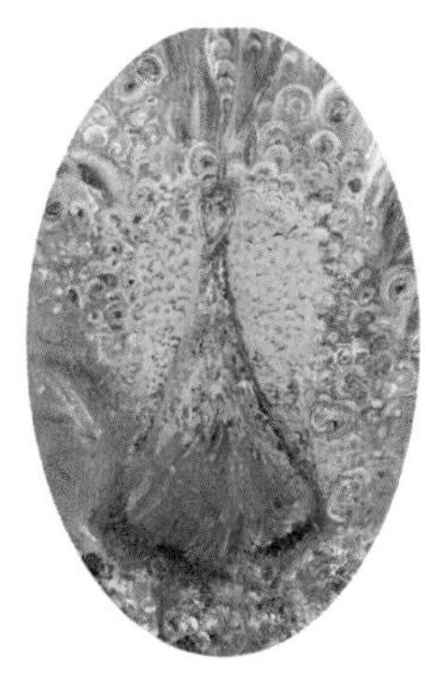

Why does a peacock have so many "eyes" on its magnificent tail?

The peacock needs to intimidate other peacocks, since it wishes to win the heart of the female.

Eyes!

IF I WERE A BUTTERFLY

If I were a caterpillar,
I would feast on leaves all day,
crawl with my many legs,
secretly plan tricks to play.

Inside my cocoon,
I'd sleep and dream
of a loving breeze
and a silent stream.

And what would I become?
Surely you all know.
I'd become a butterfly,
shining in the morning glow.

No butterfly would be as beautiful as me.
Throughout the fields, I'd wander joyfully free.

Maybe in reality I am merely a child.
But in my imagination, I can wander wild.

"Maybe in reality, I am merely a child.
But in my imagination, I can wander wild."

Maybe in my imagination I can be a/an…

My butterfly!

SECRET FRIENDSHIP

Sweet little bird, reveal your secret to me.
Your friend for a moment I'd love to be.
Without doubt, in a moment you'll soar to abandon.
Then, my Garden of Eden shall be merely a garden.

In a moment you'll discover the world from above.
And me, to defy gravity I sure would love.
My roots to the ground are deeply planted.
And my horizon is closely bounded.

I wish I could sit next to you on a bud,
soon soaring freely to roam.
We'd look at the path to my home on the ground,
but know that the world is our home.

How birds navigate during migration is a mystery. Maybe they use the location of the sun or the moon to help guide them. Maybe they migrate by using the earth's magnetic field. Some birds inhabit the same nests they used the year before when they return to their homelands.

I love my secret friend, who is…

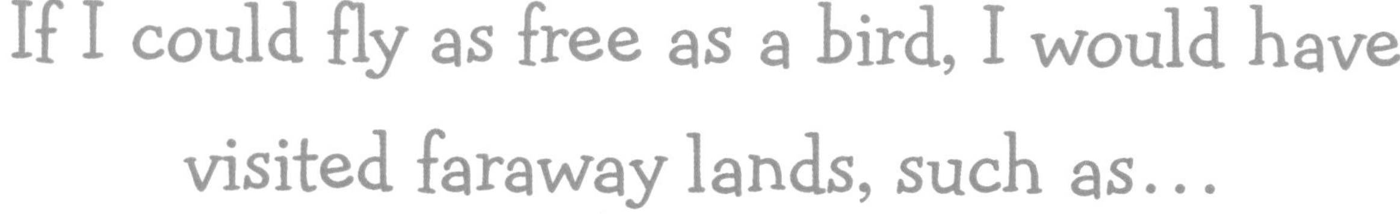
If I could fly as free as a bird, I would have visited faraway lands, such as…

Born to Be Free!

Freedom

WHY DO TREES NEED BIRDS?

We all know that birds need trees. But do trees need birds?

Why do birds need trees?

They need trees not only for shelter but also for food.

However, when a bird reaches the tree's flower to taste the nectar, or simply arrives by accident, the bird's feathers carry pollen from one part of the flower to another, causing a fruit to grow out of the flower.

Is it possible that the tree could benefit even more from what the bird does?

When the bird feeds on the tree's fruit, it is likely that it would prefer not to eat the seeds hidden inside the fruit.

Fruit is usually sweet so that animals will want to feed on it. The seeds, on the other hand, are usually bitter so that the animals will get rid of them.

Hopefully, the bird has flown away from the tree and left the seeds behind it at a distance.

If the bird swallowed the seeds, there's a good chance that the seeds will go through the bird's digestive system and reach new ground, whole and safe.

I know this is not something we like to picture in our minds, but it certainly is an effective method of spreading seeds. This gives the seeds chances to bud and eventually develop into other trees.

Continuity is the name of the game.

A tree and a bird of my own!

THE DAWN OF A SMILE AT THE HEIGHTS

As darkness comes to the forest at night,
we're hiding with such lighthearted delight
in treetops with no room for flight.

Gathering closely we celebrate night,
secretly waiting for the brightening light.
The sounds and the shadows make us unite.

You wouldn't believe the festivity of first light.
We concert our tweets as the forest shines bright.
We're cheering the first to fly high like a kite.

Do you think being a parrot is fun? You're right.
Have a wish to fly free? It's great, all right!
Smile, think free, and reach your height!

Parrots have curved bills. They can crack nuts with them. They also use them to hold onto tree branches as they move across treetops in the forest. Flying can be difficult among the mass of green foliage.

My parrot!

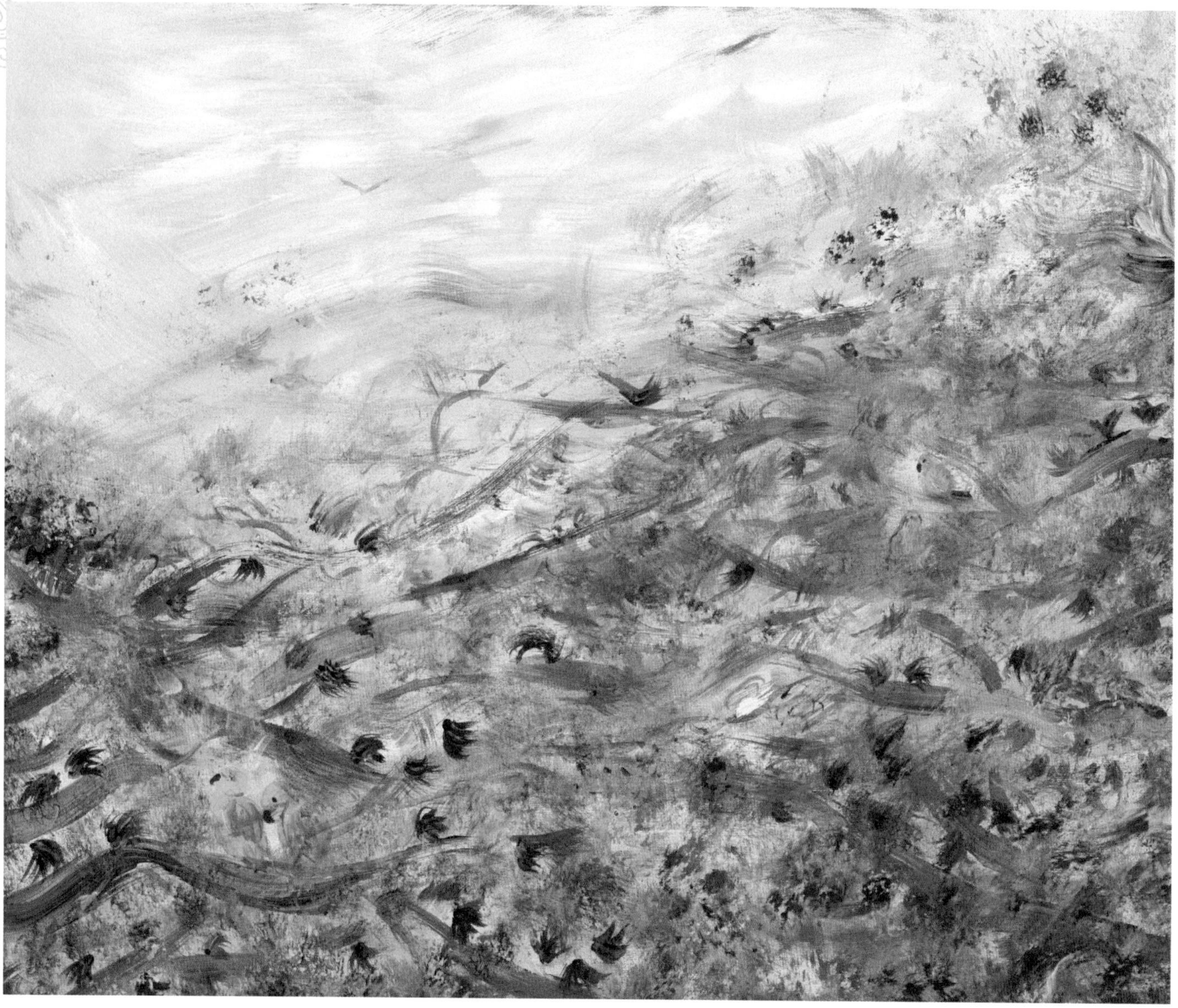

To be a free parrot is...

COLORING THE PARROTS IN RED AND GREEN?

What would you say if I suggest coloring the parrots using mostly red and green? Sounds shocking, doesn't it?

Red and green are colors that contrast. Yet they also complement each other. Together they create a dramatic effect.

Sometimes when we paint, we feel like the painting is not finished—that there's something missing in it.

If the painting is mostly red, and we add some green, it can make us feel that it's finished. We'd also feel that the painting is finished, if we color something red, and add its shadow in green.

Red is a primary color. Green is not. Green is made by mixing the two other primary colors, blue and yellow.

It is the same with the two other color couples: blue and orange (red + yellow), and yellow and purple (red + blue).

Now, what about coloring the parrots twice, each time with one of those pairs of colors? It's okay to use other colors, but use them as little as possible.

It can also be interesting to color the parrots twice with the same color combination. For example, one pair of parrots could be red, and the background could be green, while the second pair of parrots could be green, and the background could be red.

I hope you have a lot of fun experimenting. You will see the effects of this in your future works of art.

I love to play with colors...

LOTS OF BRAINS IN LITTLE HEADS

I'm sure many of you who have a dog or a cat will say that pets are extremely intelligent. There is no way I'm going to argue with that. But did you know that parrots are also very intelligent?

How do we know that parrots are intelligent?

Yes, I know; they can pronounce words—at least a few words, anyway.

But I'm sure people who have a parrot as a pet would claim they understand it, and vice versa, even if it's not a talking parrot.

Lots of brains in those little heads.

If you decide to have a parrot as a pet, you need to be careful. Certain children can develop pneumonia if they live close to parrots for a long time.

I would like to recommend adopting another bird: the zebra finch. You can find out more about this sweet, tiny bird in the next story.

WHAT DO YOU THINK? I'M A ZEBRA FINCH!

Generous beams of early sunshine lit the sparkling colors of the endless fields. The beams filtered through the trees' foliage, painting earth and flowers, as the endless green waved in the cool breeze.

So cold, thought Fun the zebra finch to himself. So alone. He looked far ahead, as if to see the rising sun beyond the horizon, hoping it would bring warmth and comfort and maybe even a friend.

With a slight swish of leaves, a beam of light lit the red and purple flowers as a parrot showed up, flying straight to the treetop.

"Hey!" Fun cried out after him in desperate joy. "I'm so glad to see you! Come down here. There's a fantastic breakfast of seeds here."

The parrot seemed to have heard something. He looked downward, as if searching for what made the sounds. Then he simply used his legs and his bill to majestically wander the treetop among the leaves and shadows.

Oh, no! thought Fun to himself. He didn't hear me crying out. He didn't even notice me. It's so hard to be a tiny bird. It's so frustrating to be so small.

Fun considered flying up to the treetop. Maybe he'd be able to make friends with the parrot after all. But sadness glued his legs to the bud as silence surrounded him. He could only hear the parrot's movements above, and that made Fun's soul silent as well.

The skies were telling a morning story in bright blue while a brave sunbeam sent smiling kisses. But Fun's loneliness and despair became a bubbling rage. The fields were lovely and lively, but Fun's heart withered in solitude.

What does this parrot think? Does he think that I'm nothing because I'm smaller than he is? What does he think? I'm a zebra finch! I'll show him what we small birds are made of.

Fun spread his wings and flew to the treetop. He began to irritate the parrot by touching the tips of his wings to the parrot's feathers over and over again.

"Hey, go away!" cried the parrot in rage. "What an irritating bird! Go, go, go!"

Fun lost his courage, and he flew to a lower bud. There were so many shadows casting away light at the treetop.

As he rested his feet and wings, a song came out of his bill. It was a song of sadness. But the caressing sounds welcomed a warming breeze. And with it, the parrot landed next to him.

"You know, before, you were annoying me out of a peaceful daydream. But that...that was some beautiful singing! Please go on. It'll be fun to welcome this morning by listening to you!"

"Hey!" Fun sparkled in delight, glowing in the morning bright. "What did you think? After all, I'm Fun, the zebra finch!"

So, dear children, what do you say about that?

Sometimes we really want something with all of our hearts. We can try to get it by behaving in an annoying, childish manner. We'd probably fail. There is a chance we'd succeed. But then we'd have what we want, with shame hanging over us.

But we could try to get what we want by positive, mature behavior. Again, we may fail. But if we succeed, we will get what we want, and feel pride straightening our backs.

The zebra finch is a sweet little bird, with origins mainly in Australia. It's a songbird that people like to raise.
It is only the male bird that sings to find his way into the heart of the female.

You can raise a male and a female together in a large enough cage, with a straw basket for the birds to create their nest. Observing their relationship and listening to the singing will give you joy.

If you want some peace and quiet at night, simply cover the birds' cage with a piece of cloth. It's quite possible they'll get the message.

My sweet zebra finch!

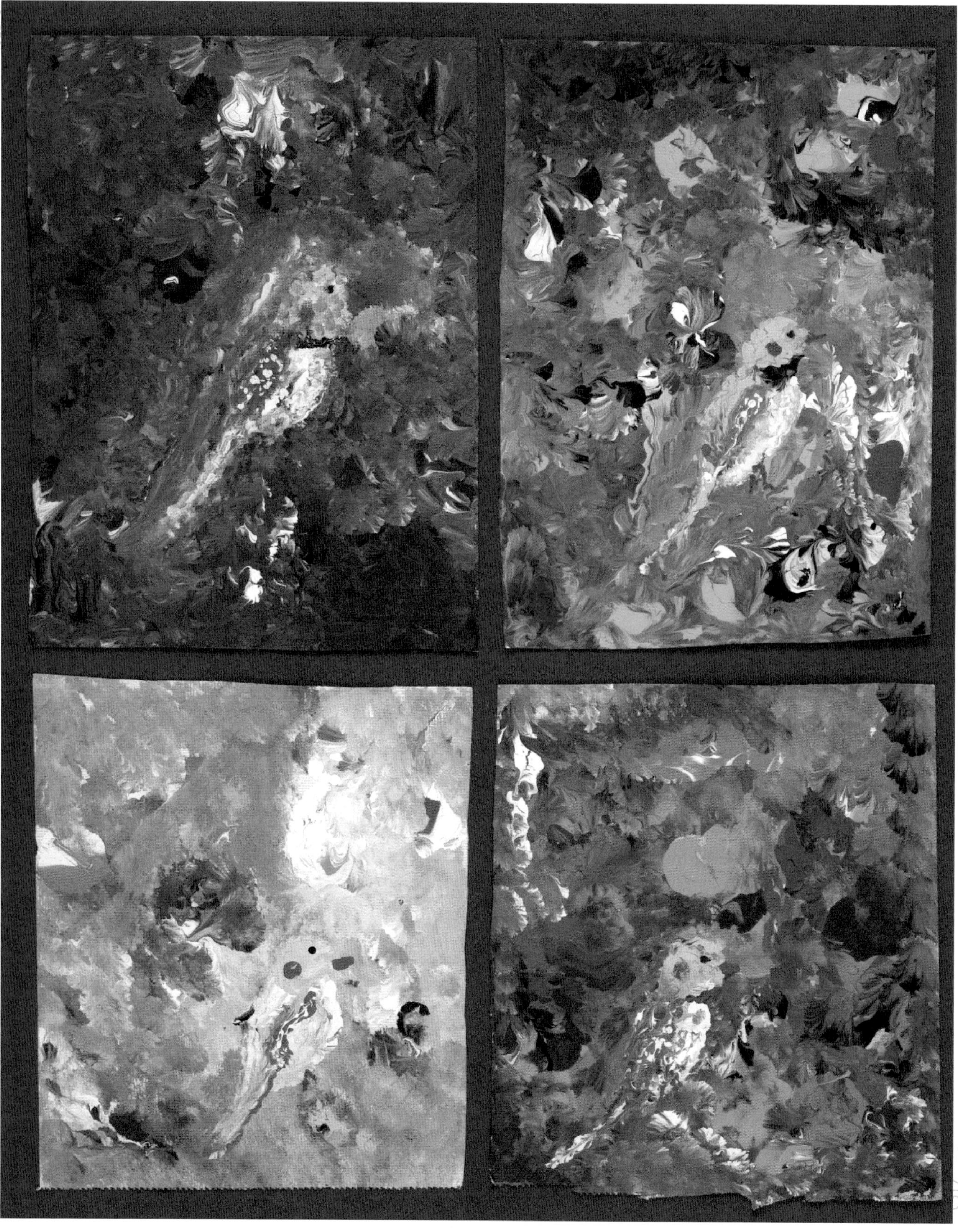

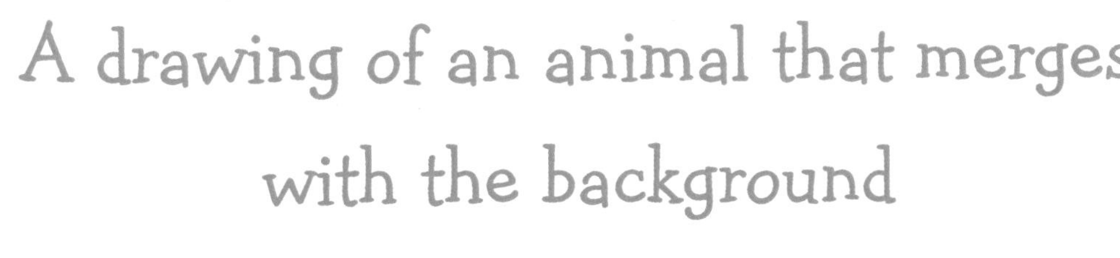

A drawing of an animal that merges with the background

WHAT STORIES DO COLORS TELL?

Why do certain animals have the colors of their surrounding environments, while others have prominent colors that make them noticeable?

Do you think the lion, the cat, the peacock, the bee, the parrot, and the zebra finch blend into their surroundings?

A lion needs to look like its surroundings so that the animal it's after won't notice it. The lion's colors camouflage it so that it will be able to get its food. However, the colors of the lion's prey camouflage it so that it will be protected from the predator.

The peacock has striking colors. It would rather risk being recognizable in its surroundings, and it carries a heavy tail in order to impress females.

Do people also make things harder on themselves and uncomfortable for themselves in order to impress the opposite gender?

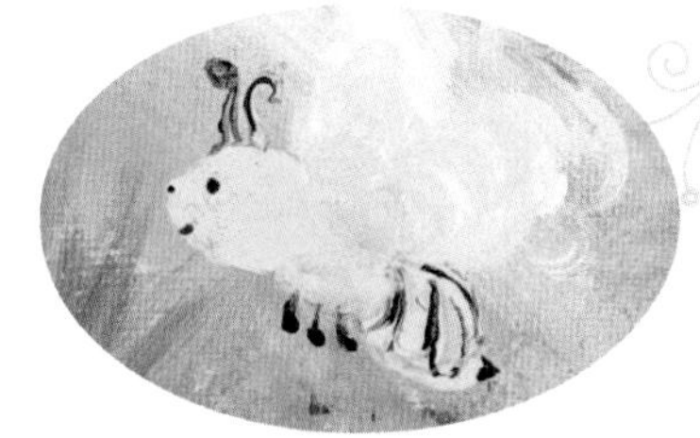

The bee has striking colors as well: yellow and black. However, the female worker bees don't need to impress the males. The males are the ones that try to impress only the queen bee.

The colors of the bee are a way of telling the attacker to beware. The attacker sees the black and yellow of the bee as a warning. It understands that the bee may attack, so it retreats. The warning colors save the bee the need to use its stinger.

Here's the painting *With First Light*. The colors of the parrots are admired as prominent and strikingly beautiful. But the parrots in the painting seem to blend into the background. Why is that? What do you think is the purpose of the parrots' colors?

The striking colors of the parrot are meant to camouflage, or hide, them, since they live in the rain forest—a colorful yet dangerous environment.

Now what about the colors of the zebra finch? What would you consider them to be? Camouflage colors, warning colors, or courting colors?

Here are some facts to take into consideration while you think about this question. The female zebra finch is gray, while the male is much more colorful. It's a bird that inhabits forests and bushes.

I wish I was colorful like

the____________________, so that...

SUCH A HEART

My face is shaped like a heart.
My heart is warm and tender.
It's as if we'll never part.
I'm loyal to you forever.

So give your heart to me,
and we'll cuddle like there's no tomorrow.
We'll share a touch, a glance, a smile,
and continue the day without sorrow.

Please mold your heart like mine.
Have you tried it, ever?
Be empathetic. Smile!
Think you'll regret it? Never!

Dear Children,

Perhaps once upon a time a little caveman child decided to adopt a stray wolf pup. Maybe it happened differently.
But the result was the same. The caveman began to raise wolves. They helped him with hunting and protecting the cave.

Today's dogs are descendants of the wolves that the cavemen domesticated.

Sometimes a wolf mother leaves her pups a piece of meat so that they'll "attack" it to prepare themselves for hunting as grown wolves.

When you leave your shoes or socks on the floor, your dog thinks you've left them there for him to use them to prepare for hunting.

So, if your dog is chewing on your shoes, socks, or anything else, he's exercising hunting like a wolf pup.

That's why I always recommend giving the dog an old shoe that would be just his on which to chew.

My puppy

A SMILE FOR ONLY YOU

Independence is my middle name.
I come and I go without shame.
Want to try me to tame?
You're going to fail at this game.

At a ball of wool I aim.
It's prey. It's quite the same.
My fur glows like a flame.
I'm clever. That's my fame.

But my heart is truly all yours.
If you think I'm loyal, you're right.
You're welcome to endlessly caress my fur
for your comfort and delight.

The cat is a distant relative of tigers and lions. Lions rub themselves on each other all the time to leave their smell on the other members of their family. It's a means of communication.

When your cat rubs itself against your pants, it wishes to leave its smell on them. This way it marks you as its family. When your pants are clean after being washed in the laundry, the cat simply has to start all over again, rubbing itself and leaving its smell. But have you ever heard any complaints?

My kitten is so...

A DOMESTICATED MOUSE?

Man chose to domesticate the wolf, from which today's dogs are descendants.

This was probably a very smart and useful decision, as the domesticated wolves helped with guarding humans and herding cattle.

It probably helped the caveman to develop his life even more.

There are animals that man didn't choose to live closely with, but adapted to living in the surroundings of man themselves.

Man must have chosen wolves (and then dogs) that were the most loyal, the most communicative, and the most responsive.

The owners of a dog can probably understand it at a single glance. The dog responds to their smallest gestures.

I'm not sure why man domesticated the cat.
I suppose wildcats were good at guarding territory, but they were also very unique pets.

But I'm sure today's cat owners will justifiably claim that caressing a cat's fur is good for one's health. And cats are such clean creatures. All day long, they engage themselves in their licking baths.

Why do you think people domesticated cats? I'm sure you have some really interesting thoughts on the subject. Well, maybe they simply had problems with mice.

Mice are a species that adapted to living with people. They learned to feed themselves on people's leftovers.

Many of you will probably raise an eyebrow if I refer to the mouse as an herbivore. I can hear you asking, "Hey, doesn't the mouse eat cheese?"

Well, the mouse does, since it has adapted itself to living in the surroundings of people and feeding off their leftovers. But in the wild, a mouse is an herbivore that feeds off the plants of its surroundings.

A domesticated mouse

A House Mouse—A Mouse House

HONEY: THE BEE WHO WANTED TO FLY

Once upon a time, there was a small beehive. Actually, from the outside it seemed small. Inside, it was like a very large city with many little rooms called cells. And thousands of bees lived there.

One day the queen bee traveled from cell to cell, and she laid a tiny egg in each one. When she was finished, she went to rest. Now the worker bees tended to the rest of the chores.

After about three days, a larva had hatched out of each egg. All day long, bees traveled thousands of times from cells of honey, nectar, and pollen to the cells of the larvae to feed them.

A few days later, the larvae pupated. Inside each cocoon, a miracle happened. The larvae became bees.

One of them was Honey. While she was transforming, she dreamed of flying far away and discovering the world. When she woke up, she hurried to the exit of the hive and spread her wings as quickly as she could.

However, a worker bee named Tidy quickly came over and said to her, "Where are you going? You've just become a bee, and you think you can fly away from the nest? First you need to learn all the tasks of the hive."

"And when I do, will I be able to fly away?" asked Honey hopefully.

"Yes," replied Tidy, "when you're older. Right now, you just can't!"

For the first days of her life as a worker bee, all Honey had to do was feed the larvae. As the tedious work went on and on, she fantasized about flying far away.

One morning while she was daydreaming at work, Tidy came to her and said, "Honey, it's time for you to try flying!"

"Oh! That's wonderful!" Honey cried out. Enthusiastically, she approached the exit of the nest and spread her wings. But flying was so difficult that she landed quickly inside.

"That's okay," Tidy comforted her. "It'll become easier."

Honey's next chore was to build new cells for the larvae and for the storage of pollen, nectar, and honey. Then she got a new job, guarding the entrance of the hive.

One day, when she was tired of guarding the nest, Tidy came to her and said, "That's it, Honey. You're all grown up now. You've practiced all the tasks of the hive. From now on, you'll be a forager. You'll be gathering pollen and nectar."

Honey was thrilled. She laughed and buzzed, "It's such a wonderful, perfect day. I'm finally going to fly away!"

Honey approached the exit of the nest. The light of the glowing sun dazzled her for a moment. She felt as if the sun was shining especially for her. She spread her wings and flew as far away as she could.

Honey enjoyed the clear, fragrant wind. She landed on a sweet-smelling purple flower. She gathered pollen into the small pollen basket that was on her hind legs. Honey savored the delicious nectar and hummed:

"Such an interesting journey it turned out to be.
Be joyful and marvel at life, just like me."

The Perfect Day

My most perfect day ever!

THE BEE NEST: NOT A PLACE TO REST

There is so much to be done inside a beehive: feeding the larvae, building new cells, guarding the entrance to the nest, and so much more. How do the bees know what chore to do?

The bee goes through stages in its life. Each new stage presents it with its next chore, as described in our story "Honey: The Bee Who Wanted to Fly."

Often, when I tell this story to children, a child suddenly rises and passionately asks, "And in the end, does she fly away?"

I'm sure you've identified with this feeling of being young and inexperienced with life.

We wish to take responsibility over our lives, but we have to be looked after by the adults until we're ready and we know more about the world.

Well, there is time to grow, and there is time to glow.

Being taken care of by a responsible adult, as we grow, allows us to glow with the magic of childhood today.

Being able to go out to the world only when we're mature and ready, will allow us to glow then.

I guess what's important is to accept the stage you're in, and to see its bright side. The time to be independent, mature, and responsible will come, as it did for Honey.

Here's something interesting about the grown bees:
If a bee finds a field of flowers full of nectar, it will return to the hive and communicate with the other bees through a "round dance" if the field is close to the beehive, or a "waggle dance" if it's farther away. The foragers will know where to find the field, based on the dance.

When the sun is shining, I feel...

A RAINBOW OF COLORS

What's the connection between light, animals that can see at night, and the bee?

How can you split the light into its color components easily at home?

What you need is a CD—the kind you use with your computer—or a DVD. All you need to do is turn the disc upside down and turn on a lamp of white light.

The white light is consisted of the spectrum of all colors.
The disc like a prism disperses the white light into its color components.

When the rays of the sun's light pass through raindrops, a beautiful spectacle is displayed in the sky.

What's the name for it?

You're right – a rainbow.

Are we able to see the whole range of the rainbow's spectrum of colors? Unfortunately, we're not. We can't see in the ultraviolet and the infrared ranges. But certain animals can.

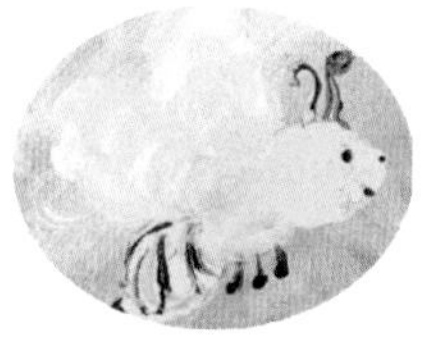

Some flowers have ultraviolet "traffic signs" for forager bees, directing them to the nectar.

The ultraviolet in the light of the sun is not visible to people. But we still need to be aware of those rays, since they could burn our skins, if we tried to get a tan when the sun is high in the sky.

Why are we advised to get a tan early in the morning or late in the afternoon? At those times, the beams of the sun reach the ozone layer diagonally, traveling a longer path through it. The ultraviolet rays are thus better filtered, so we are better protected.

To which animal is the infrared light visible?

Finding food during the day can be very problematic for a snake. It doesn't have any legs. The sun warms the ground. If the snake tries to crawl, it will probably fry itself.

A logical solution is to look for food at night. But how will the snake be able to find the little animal it's after?

Are our bodies warm? You can easily check this out by taking your own temperature. Even when we're not running a fever, our bodies' temperatures are quite high. The bodies of the little animals are warm, too.

When they run around at night, the little animals can be detected by snakes, which have sensors for infrared light.

Now let's go back to the rainbow.

What shape is the rainbow? Actually, the rainbow's shape is a full circle. The bottom of the rainbow meets the earth. Therefore, we don't see it. Have you ever seen a rainbow from an airplane?

The colors of the rainbow that are visible to people are red, orange, yellow, green, blue, indigo (blue violet), and violet—in that order, from top to bottom.

Why not color the rainbow drawing with pastel crayons? These crayons are oil based. You will be able to merge the different colors where they meet by brushing a finger over them. The effect will be spectacular!

My rainbow!

A RAINBOW OF MORE THAN SEVEN COLORS?

**Here are some more interesting facts about light.
The primary colors of light are red, green, and blue. Are you confused? Where did yellow go?**

Yes, I know. One of the first things we are taught is that the primary colors are red, yellow, and blue. By mixing them, we'll get all the colors we need in order to color and paint.

When we refer to the primary colors of light—which are red, green, and blue—we talk about creating colored light.

The primary colors of light are called additive primaries, because each color added to the light adds to the illumination (RGB: red, green, and blue).

This is easy to demonstrate.

We can simply take three flashlights and cover one with red cellophane, the second with green, and the third with blue. We will probably need about three layers of cellophane on each flashlight. What's important is that the three flashlights are the same. The quantity of cellophane on each flashlight should be the same, too.

What will happen if we direct the three flashlights to the same spot on a white ceiling or wall? Will we get black?

No. The additive primaries will add to each other, and we'll see the color white.
We can have some more fun with the flashlights.

How can we create yellow light?

When the light of the red flashlight and the light of the green one meet on a white wall or ceiling, what we get is **yellow**—a secondary color of the light.

The red light and the blue light will produce a color called magenta (bright purplish red).

The blue light and the green light will produce cyan (a sort of turquoise).

We are lucky, since our eyes have receptors for three colors: red, green, and blue. Our eyes combine those three colors to create the colorful image of the world as we see it.

However, the butterfly, for instance, is much luckier.
Its eyes have receptors for five to six colors.

We can only imagine all the shades of colors it sees in one image made up of these colors.

When a butterfly looks at a rainbow in the sky, many more shades of colors are visible to it, than to people. What's more, the ultraviolet, invisible to us, is visible to this tiny beautiful creature.

It sure is lucky!

And what about red, yellow, and blue—the primary colors we use to color and paint?
Let's say we cover a flashlight with about three layers of red cellophane. Only red color is transmitted through the cellophane, which serves as a filter.

The white light is consisted of the spectrum of all colors, remember? But they are subtracted from it by the filter, except for the color red.

We can add the same quantity of yellow and blue cellophane to the red cellophane already covering the flashlight.

Then the three subtractive primary colored filters don't allow any color to be transmitted through them. All the colors the white light is consisted of are subtracted from it. That's why we call those primary colors *subtractive primaries* (RYB: red, yellow, and blue).

The rainbow as the butterfly sees it

THE GLOW OF A MORNING STROLL

Once I saw in the sand a hole.
From which popped up a soul with a goal.
On the sand, she enthusiastically traveled.
Clearly, at the glow of the landscape, she marveled.

"What's your name?" I asked. "Be true."
She suddenly stopped. "What's it matter to you?
I'm gathering grain. I have so much to do!
"You, big guy, should be more industrious, too!"

"But I know who you are," I proudly said.
"You're an ant. Why work? Come play instead!"
She looked at me and solemnly replied,
"Look, it's as if a clock's ticking in my mind.
Prepare for winter!
If I don't gather food and go play instead,
How will the ants in the winter be fed?"

I blushed. My cheeks became all red.
"You're right. Go gather food," I said.

Dear Children,

Maybe you were confused by the description of the ant as a soul. Well, the ant is an animal, and in Latin, *animalis* means having breath or soul.

The ants prepare all summer for winter. Ants can carry food that is heavier than their own weight. They gather food in storage rooms along the tunnels of their nests. Their persistence and community organization are amazing.

Once I saw in the sand a hole, from which…

AN EYE AT THE TIP OF A FEATHER

Hi. Look me straight in the eye.
Don't be intimidated.
I only like to intimidate other peacocks,
Who naturally aren't as strong and healthy as I am.

Yesterday I dressed up. It was very easy.
I simply spread my tail feathers.
I had eyes for a beautiful female peacock.
She was gray and certainly didn't have a tail like mine.
But that was for the best.
Gray is a color of camouflage—important for a mother who's protecting her chicks.

Still, she was the apple of my eye.
I danced around her and sang,
"Hi. Look me straight in the eye!"
Unfortunately, she looked straight at the eye at
the tip of the third feather on the left in my tail.

Anyhow, she saw how colorful and glowing my
feathers were. She concluded that since I must be
strong and healthy, so will my chicks be.

She said, "Hi, handsome!"
Now I'm no longer lonesome.

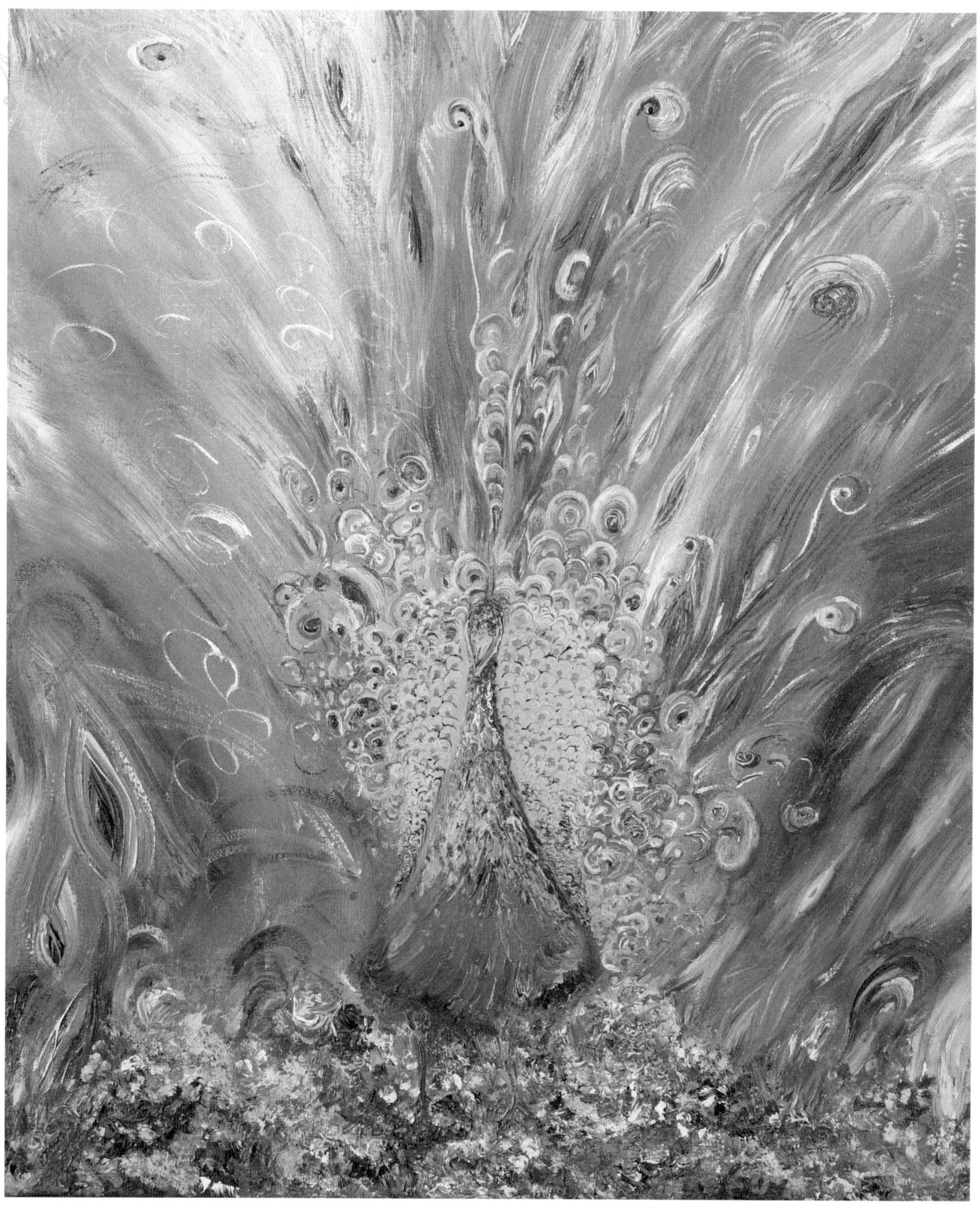

Eyes from Fairy Tales

A fairy tale about the peacock...

The Peacock, Inspired by Brazil's Carnivals

Dancing makes me feel...

Glow: The White Peacock

Dear Children,

As you see, I just love painting peacocks. Would you like to draw a peacock too? Don't worry. You'll have a chance very soon. A white peacock does exist. Look for its pictures.

My peacock

SYMMETRY: IT'S NOT ONLY A MATTER OF BEAUTY

Why does the female peacock choose the peacock whose tail is not only the most beautiful and the most colorful, but also whose tail feathers are the most symmetric?

Do people observe symmetry that easily?
Do we also prefer symmetrical faces or objects?

Why is it important?

When the peacock dances around the female to court her, she can determine within moments if his feathers are totally symmetric.

Nature gave her this tool to figure out if the peacock is healthy or not. A peacock whose genes are not of health will have tail feathers that are not totally symmetric. What's more, his colors will be dull.

So, based on the male peacock's outer appearance, the female can determine his state of health. This is very important. If she chooses the healthiest male, her offspring will carry those genes.

Continuity is the name of the game.

People also observe whether a face is symmetrical in a split second. For us, a beautiful face will be a symmetrical one. Why do you think we have this preference?

When cavemen wandered the woods, it was crucial to observe a predator as soon as possible. A predator had a symmetrical face: its eyes were at the front of its face symmetrically.

Cavemen developed an ability to notice symmetrical faces quickly so they could notice danger among the shadows of the forests as soon as possible.

People's bodies and faces are symmetrical, too: we have two hands, two legs, two ears, two eyes, and so on. The right sides of our bodies are symmetrical with the left sides.

Perceiving symmetry is something we've inherited from the cavemen. We prefer symmetry as an indicator of health. However, for us, this has become an aesthetic preference, too. Symmetrical faces and objects simply look more beautiful to us.

What would happen if the pictures on the walls of your living room would not hang straight? How long would you and your family members be able to tolerate it?

How would you feel talking to someone whose glasses did not sit straight on his face? Would you be able to concentrate on what that person was saying? I'm afraid we prefer bilateral symmetry.

You can have fun creating symmetry. Take a sheet of paper and lay some patches of different acrylic colors on it. Blend the colors a bit. Looks a bit like a mess, doesn't it?

Now try to fold the paper into two identical parts. Simply lay the right side on the left side of the paper. Then open the folded paper. Your work of art now has bilateral symmetry. It looks somewhat more harmonious and more appealing to our eyes, doesn't it?

There are other sorts of symmetry.

One is translational symmetry.

The drawing of the peacock translates, or repeats, itself over and over again.

Then there is reflection symmetry.

How does it feel to color a drawing that faces right and then left? It looks like a reflection in a mirror.

When I look at myself in the mirror, I…

THE CHUBBY CUB AND THE CHILD OF COURAGE

Lend me your ears. I have a story of courage and bravery and loyalty for you.

Let's travel the world afar, through time, through forests, over hills, and along rivers that forever rhyme.

At the entrance to a tepee—an Indian tent—stands a child alone. His eyes sparkle with blue; his mouth is caught in a frown. His stance is defiant. He's Bear Cub, the chief of the tribe's son. Taming his tears, he watches an approaching man.

"Light Through Clouds," he whispers. "You always cure illness. Please tell me that my father is going to overcome his sickness!"

Light Through Clouds caresses the timid boy's cheek. "You have the tenacity of a young bear, Bear Cub. You were named properly. I'm afraid the time to test your courageous heart is to come very soon. The wind of the forest struck your father. Usually, the forest gives me herbs to heal. But not this time."

"But surely there's something I can do!" the boy cries out. "Well," says Light Through Clouds, while watching the sunset

among foliage thick as a bear's fur. "Last night, I consulted the spirits in dreams clear of mist. There's only one thing that can heal your father: the sweetest and purest honey you've ever tasted.

"In the wonder of dreams, I've seen a hive far in the mountains and beyond the wide river. There, the eagles soar over stonewalled ravines. The hive awaits you there, in a clearing of trees, surrounded by bees surfing the breeze.
If only your father could taste this healing honey."

Bear Cub had already made up his mind. "There's no time to waste!"

But the sun has already taken its light away and gone to sleep. Bear Cub has to wait for the light to return before he can begin his trip.

That night, around the shimmering fire, a whole community dances and sings as one.

"Tomorrow I will go strong. My heart will beat with courage as if all your hearts drum inside me," assures Bear Cub. "And don't worry. I am not going alone."

And when the first light of dawn colors the horizon, Bear Cub peeks through the entrance of a cave. Tucked in a cushion of leaves sleeps a real bear cub. He opens his eyes, surprised to find his friend.

"Hey, boy, long time no see. What's on your mind?"

"My father is not well," the boy whispers. "I need your help!"

"Sure." The bear cub is already standing up, giving the child a true bear hug.

"We need to travel deep into the forest," the child manages to say, caving into the hug and kisses of his jumbo furry friend.

"The forest?" The bear cub releases the child as he leaps in delight.

"Yes," continues the boy, "we need to bring my father the purest healing honey you've ever tasted."

"Honey? Oh, dear, I'm having this craving for something sweet, as I've been sleeping all winter. Tell me, has the snow frosted?"

"The paths are as brown as your fur," the child says in amusement and enchantment.

"And when we reach this hive, can I have some of this fine, fine honey for myself?" yearns the bear.

"Well, okay," says the boy, "but only when we've filled this bottle with it for my dad."

"Come on, then!" The bear is already out. "Oh, the sun!" His eyes sparkle in delight. "I just love the morning bright."

And so, a bear and a boy, both young in body and spirit, begin their journey, finding their way through the well-known paths of the forest, leaping in confident strides over stones that cross the wide river.

They walk in silence across unknown ground, counting only on their instincts and defiance. The eagles direct them from above until the bear and the boy reach a secret path, seen only by those who are on a journey to heal someone they love.

All of a sudden, the path, which has been covered in plants and flowers, opens to a clearing bathed in sunlight. An old tree rises in the middle, its old, wrinkled trunk rooted to earth and land.

"Oh, no!" The boy reaches the tree. "I can't take the honey out of the hive. The bees will sting me. We've made this entire journey for nothing."

"Relax!" The young bear rests his hip on the tree, showing off his paw with pride and bragging without shame. "Have you ever seen such a beautiful, rugged, furry paw? A bee's sting can do me no harm."

As he brags, he dives his paw into the hive and then pulls it out, dripping with shiny honey that blushes in heartening sunlight.

The journey back is easier for the body but not for the spirit. The young bear feels the child's restlessness. The boy prepares himself to face his father, holding onto his and to his community's hope that he can heal the worshipped chief.

As they reach the village, they say their farewells.

"Hey, don't worry. Don't be tight," shouts the bear, his run light as a flight. "I'll come to you in dreams of night."
He waves his paw, all furry, and runs off in a hurry.

As the boy sets his feet on the village's main path, the people dare to hope that he'd cast out the spirits' wrath.

He walks the path with courage only a bear cub can inspire. His silent stride is soft, but his heart feels like it's on fire.

Bear Cub enters the tent, accompanied by a beam of light, and kneels before his father, hoping to do right.

"Father, please sip this pure, healing honey!" he begs.

The father, his face wrinkled like a trunk of a tree, sips the medicine that only his child could bring.

Hope that the journey bears fruit begins to take root in the young child's mind. He gazes with awe at his father, who is one of a kind.

"Child," the father says as his face brightens and begins to bloom, "You're my heart's groom. You've cast away my gloom."

I'm a Native American Child, Too!

Dear Children,

First, do you have, or did you use to have, a teddy bear? Why do children all over the world hug a teddy bear before going to sleep?

Well, it's rooted in the fact that, for Native Americans, the bear symbolized vigor. It inspired them with courage and gave them peace of mind. Aren't courage and peace of mind exactly what your teddy bear gives you?

Secondly, have you ever wondered about the source of the common belief that the bear likes honey? The bear feeds on sweet, nutritious food before going to sleep through winter. It prepares to hibernate by eating honey and decaying fruit.

And lastly, did you know that when America was discovered, the Native Americans grew nutritious plants unknown to the Europeans, such as corn, potatoes, and tomatoes?

IN THE SHADE OF AN OLD TREE

In the shade of a solemn old tree that had seen a lot, there was a huge elephant. He used his trunk to tear off leaves from branches. Then he peacefully chewed on the leaves. He seemed to be somewhat bored.

On the warm sand a few feet away, there was a tiny mouse, munching on leaves of a small plant.

All of a sudden, a meowing was heard. The mouse cried out, "Oh, no, a...cat! Dad, Mom, help!" Soon, running fast as the wind, the little mouse disappeared.

From behind a bush, a cat appeared. "Such a shame. They always tell me that I'm arrogant, that I love hearing myself meowing. There runs off a delicious dinner."

The leaves of the tree swished, and the cat glanced up. "Maybe there's dinner here for me after all. Surely I can eat an elephant!"

Without hesitation, the cat meowed again. The elephant trumpeted in amusement and disdain.

"Okay, I get it," murmured the cat as the elephant stared with glee. "An elephant cannot be food for me."

A dog came near, showing no fear.
I'm bigger, he thought to himself with pride. I'll scare off this cat, just for the ride.

The dog, with self-confidence, began to bark.
The cat turned away and took off like a spark.

Like the whisper of wind, the cat disappeared.
The elephant, however, wagged his tail and ears.
He didn't jolt or shake with fear.

In tired, majestic strides, a lion arrived. "What's a dog doing here?" he cried. "All I wish is to be alone."
The lion roared, and the dog, like the wind, was gone.

Good, thought the lion. Now I can lie down in the shade of the tree and sweetly meditate. As he yawned, he glanced up. "Apparently, I'm not in the shade of a tree. I'm in the shade of an elephant!" the lion roared, but the elephant only got more bored.

The lion was furious. "Who does this elephant think he is? He's just an herbivore. I myself am a carnivore."

Unexpectedly, the elephant opened his mouth and said, "I see you're left here all alone. Had you not have driven the dog away, you would have had someone to play with, here in the shade. You and the dog and the cat—you should learn how to become better friends. Ask the children. They'll teach you all about good friendship!"

The lion opened his mouth. He wanted to shout. Then, with a pout, he only cried out, "You know what? You're right. I'll just go to sleep here all alone. Soon it will be night."

All along, from the beginning of this scene, a bird had hidden in the old tree unseen. "Very interesting.
The mouse escaped. So did the cat and the dog.
The lion went on sleeping alone like a log.
Both the mouse and the elephant were herbivores.
The tiny mouse ate the same,
As the elephant no one could tame.
Now I'm going to fly off and look for new adventures.
I just love new surprises and all of life's ventures."

This story depicts the food chain. The carnivore eats the herbivore. It doesn't do it out of evil, but simply because that's its food.

The herbivore eats plants—vegetables, fruit, seeds, and leaves—whatever grows on the earth in its surroundings that is right for its species.

Herbivores use their senses to detect danger. Carnivores need to focus on their prey. They use their senses in order to get their food.

The elephant, however, is so big that it doesn't have to be afraid of any animal. Humans are the ones who have done a lot of bad things to elephants. But I hear there are people whose sole purpose in life is to protect elephants from humans.

Elephants have hair that is short and scattered. An elephant's skin is thick and abrasive. If a fly rests on the back of the elephant, it doesn't bother it, since the elephant doesn't even feel it. Wouldn't we all like skin like that, so that tiny issues wouldn't irritate us?

The elephant is so big, it makes me feel...

My own food chain!

ABOUT SIGHT AND STRIPES IN BLACK AND WHITE

What would happen if you placed a finger closely in front of your nose?

No, I'm not asking you to do that while both eyes are open.

Place a finger in front of your nose, and close one eye and then the other, over and over again.

What happened to the finger?

The finger seemed to move to the right and to the left, while actually it stayed in the same place.

How can that be?

The right eye saw the finger from the right, while the left one saw it from the left.

Our brains combined what the two eyes saw into one image—a three-dimensional image.

Do carnivores have three-dimensional sight? Why?

Both of the lion's eyes are in the front of its face. It can see a three-dimensional image.

This allows the lion to focus on the herbivore animal it's after for food.

What about herbivores' sight?

Herbivore animals' eyes are on the sides of their heads. What the two eyes see is not the same. Their sight is not three-dimensional.

But those animals don't need to focus on other animals. They need to be able to see all around them in order to detect approaching predators.

Since their eyes are on the sides of their heads, they can not only see what's in front of them (even if not so well), but also what's beside them, and even what's behind them. You don't want to play hide-and-seek with an herbivore.

Imagine the blur in a lion's eyes as he's trying to focus on a zebra running the fields among an entire herd. All of the dancing stripes confuse the lion into giving up. The zebras will simply run on and on, since it's easy for them to see the lion even if it's behind them.

In such a case, the zebra would surely thank the wise protection nature gave it: stripes. And the lion? It'll just have to look for dinner elsewhere.

In conclusion, let me ask you a question: Is our vision the same as that of carnivores or herbivores?

Yes, I know: we're like the carnivores. It's not how we'd like to think of ourselves. But three-dimensional sight is spectacular. I wouldn't give it up.

NATURE'S WISE FAIR SHARE

Do You Like the Painting?

Observe it a little. Why do you think is it good that different species of animals inhabit this environment?

What would have happened if there were only elephants, or only lions? Would there be food for everybody?

I'd like to introduce a new term to you: *diversity*. This is something that is very important for the survival of animals and mankind.

A giraffe can reach higher leaves of a tree than an elephant can. The lion can eat the cat. The cat can eat the mouse, which can feed on leaves of a small bush. Isn't it wonderful? There's food for everybody.

LET'S DANCE TO THE RHYTHM

Here's something interesting that arises from "In the Shade of an Old Tree".

A band or an orchestra plays music in harmony because all of the musicians follow the same rhythm.

Do our bodies have rhythms? How can we feel them?
Put a hand on your chest in order to feel your heart, or
place a finger on your wrist in order to feel your pulse.

How many heartbeats do we have per minute?

A mouse's heart beats about five hundred times a minute. An elephant's heart, however, beats about thirty times a minute.

A mouse lives approximately four years. An elephant, on the other hand, lives fifty years.

Do you think there is a connection between these facts?

The mouse is very fast. This is connected to the fact that it has so many heartbeats per minute. Unfortunately its life is very short.

The elephant, however, is very slow. Its heart beats slowly, but it lives a longer life.

The total number of heartbeats of an elephant during its entire life is about the same as the total of heartbeats of a mouse. Interesting, isn't it?

Here's a project you might want to try. I'm sure it'll be fun. Take two transparent hoses—a very short one and a long one. Put some beads inside each hose. Then, using wide tape, connect the beginning of each hose to its end.

The short hose will demonstrate the heartbeats of the mouse. The beads have a short way to flow, like the blood in the small body of the mouse. The blood doesn't have a long way to flow through, so the heart needs to push it constantly, many times per minute.

The long hose will demonstrate the heartbeat of the elephant. The beads have a long way to flow along. And so it will take much longer for the blood of the elephant to circulate through its whole body.

Because of this, the heart of the elephant needs to beat fewer times a minute in order to push the blood.

Dear Children,

Naturally, we need to build houses to live in. But sometimes, when a field, a bush, or a forest is cleared for new houses or roads, animals that once inhabited that area cannot go on living there, as they have lost their shelter and their food.

Losing one thing in the food chain influences another. If a certain plant doesn't grow in a certain area anymore, the herbivore that fed on it cannot go on living there. Because of this, the carnivore that fed on the herbivore cannot live there anymore either.

One endangered species is the butterfly. Each species of butterfly depends on certain plants for its nutrition and for the continuity of its species. One way to attract butterflies to places inhabited by people is to find out the types of plants the butterflies that used to inhabit the area needed. All you need to do is to plant those plants.

Animal life is important for mankind. We need milk from cows, and eggs from chickens. Even the little bee is significant. Honey and other products of the beehive are nutritious.

Moreover, bees pollinate flowers. They transfer pollen from flower to flower, or within parts of a particular flower. The result of this process will be a new plant of the same kind. Continuity is the name of the game. Remember?

The plants that the earth grows are important for people as well. Many plants have not been researched yet. This means that plants from which medicines for incurable diseases could be made could become extinct.

I hope you enjoyed the stories in *Creative Children Like the Animals of the World*. Many of the animals I wrote about are in danger of extinction.

Cats and dogs are not, as they have adapted to life with people. But their relatives that live in the wild are.

I hope the book helped you to develop your creative thinking. Grow to be a **creative** adult, and you'll develop and inspire others. Grow to be a **thinker,** and you'll be aware of the animals, the plants, and the fascinating variety of people in our world.

Yours truly,
Michelle

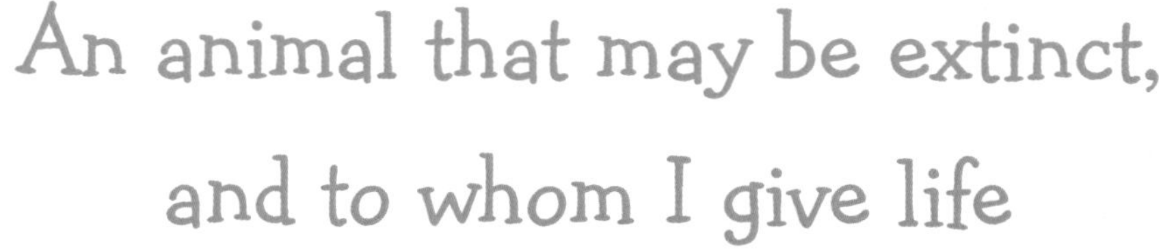

An animal that may be extinct,

and to whom I give life

A KISS GOOD NIGHT

Night kisses day,
day kisses night,
in an infinite dance
of dark and bright.

So has it been
since the dawn of time.
There's lots of time.
So go on with the rhyme.
Make the dance timeless!

With a kiss good night,
I say farewell.
The dance shall flow
as an endless well.

When day kisses night good night, I...

The Kiss

A HUG GOOD NIGHT—GOOD MORNING

I'll fall asleep hugged tight,
filled with lightheartedness.
I'll wake by beams of light
to hearty tenderness.

I'll gaze at wondrous sight.
Delight at the birth of light.
Inhale the air so bright.
Feel cuddled soft and tight.

The touch of air.
The touch of sky.
The touch of sea.
The seagulls fly.

Goes on the rhyme
beyond the time...
Goes on the rhyme
beyond the time...

Beyond the horizon there is/are...

With a kiss good night,
I say farewell.
The dance shall flow
as an endless well...

Michelle

Made in the USA
Middletown, DE
21 July 2019